OXFORD
UNIVERSITY PRESS

A Busy Morning at the Bank

Daniel McGillis

Illustrated by Mona Daly

OXFORD
UNIVERSITY PRESS

198 Madison Avenue
New York, NY 10016 USA

Great Clarendon Street, Oxford OX2 6DP UK

Oxford University Press is a department of the
University of Oxford. It furthers the University's
objective of excellence in research, scholarship,
and education by publishing worldwide in

Oxford   New York
Auckland Cape Town Dar es Salaam
Hong Kong Karachi Kuala Lumpur Madrid
Melbourne Mexico City Nairobi New Delhi
Shanghai Taipei Toronto

With offices in
Argentina Austria Brazil Chile Czech Republic
France Greece Guatemala Hungary Italy Japan
Poland Portugal Singapore South Korea
Switzerland Thailand Turkey Ukraine Vietnam

OXFORD and OXFORD ENGLISH are registered
trademarks of Oxford University Press.

Photocopying

The Publisher grants permission for the
photocopying of those pages marked
"photocopiable" according to the following
conditions. Individual purchasers may make copies
for their own use or for use by classes that they
teach. School purchasers may make copies for use
by staff and students, but this permission does not
extend to additional schools or branches.

Under no circumstances may any part of this book
be photocopied for resale.

Executive Publishing Manager: Stephanie Karras
Managing Editor: Sharon Sargent
Design Manager: Stacy Merlin
Project Coordinator: Sarah Dentry
Production Layout Artist: Colleen Ho
Cover Design: Colleen Ho, Stacy Merlin,
Michael Steinhofer
Manufacturing Manager: Shanta Persaud
Manufacturing Controller: Eve Wong

ISBN: 978 0 19474032 6 (BOOK)

ISBN: 978 0 19474039 5 (OPD READING LIBRARY)

ISBN: 978 0 19474057 9 (CIVICS READING LIBRARY)

Printed in China

10 9 8 7 6

Many thanks to Pronk&Associates, Kelly Stern,
and Meg Brooks for a job well done.

A Busy Morning at the Bank

Table of Contents

A. Match the pictures with the words.

_e_ 1. account manager

___ 2. ATM

___ 3. balance

___ 4. check

___ 5. deposit

___ 6. savings account

___ 7. teller

___ 8. withdraw

B. Answer the questions.

1. How many banks are in your neighborhood?
2. What are their names?
3. What can people do at a bank?
4. How often do you go to the bank?

C. Read the title of this book. Look at the pictures in the book. Then guess the answers to the questions. Circle *a* or *b*.

I walk into the bank and go to the counter. The teller asks, "Can I help you?"
"Yes, please," I say. I put my check on the counter. "I need to open an account and deposit this check."
"So you want to open a checking account?" the teller asks.
"Yes," I say. "I need a checking account. But I also want a savings account. Can I open both accounts today?"
"Sure," says the teller.

5

1. Where does this story happen?
   a. at a post office
   b. at a bank

2. Who is this story about?
   a. Han Na
   b. Felicia

3. What does Han Na do at the bank?
   a. open bank accounts
   b. get a new job

4. Who does Han Na meet first at the bank?
   a. a security guard
   b. a teller

3

Chapter 1

I Need Two Bank Accounts

It's Monday, and I have my first paycheck from my new job. I'm the cook at a Korean restaurant. The check says, "Pay to the order of Han Na Park."

I'm on my way to the bank on the corner. I'm going to open two bank accounts. I need a checking account so I can pay my bills. I also want a savings account. I'm saving for a trip to Korea. My sister lives there.

I walk into the bank and go to the counter. The teller asks, "Can I help you?"

"Yes, please," I say. I put my check on the counter. "I need to open an account and deposit this check."

"So you want to open a checking account?" the teller asks.

"Yes," I say. "I need a checking account. But I also want a savings account. Can I open both accounts today?"

"Sure," says the teller.

"Can I also withdraw some cash today?" I ask.

"Yes, you can," says the teller. "You need to see an account manager. I can take you to Mr. Lombardi. He can help you open your new accounts."

"Thank you, Felicia," I say.

"You know my name!" she says. Then she laughs. "Of course! I'm wearing my name tag. And your name is Han Na Park. It says that on your check."

Felicia brings me to Mr. Lombardi's desk.

"Dominic, this is Han Na Park," says Felicia. "She wants to open a checking account. She also needs a savings account."

Felicia turns to me. "This is Dominic Lombardi, one of our account managers," she says.

"Hello, Ms. Park," says Mr. Lombardi. "Please sit down."

I sit down on a chair in front of his desk. Felicia leaves.

Is this going to be difficult? I wonder.

A. Mark the sentences T (true) or F (false).

_F_ 1. Han Na needs a job.

___ 2. Han Na has a checking account.

___ 3. Han Na wants some cash.

___ 4. Felicia opens an account for Han Na.

___ 5. Han Na meets the account manager.

B. Choose *a* or *b*.

1. People deposit ___ in the bank.
   - (a.) checks
   - b. accounts

2. A ___ works in a bank.
   - a. teller
   - b. customer

3. When you need money, you ___ it.
   - a. deposit
   - b. withdraw

4. You should pay your bills with your ___.
   - a. savings account
   - b. checking account

5. The ___ helps people open accounts.
   - a. account manager
   - b. cook

C. Organize information. Complete the chart. Use the words in the box.

an account manager	a check	a checking account
a cook	a counter	~~deposit a check~~
open an account	a teller	withdraw cash

Actions	People	Things
deposit a check		

What's going to happen next? What do you think? Read the question. Then circle your guess, *yes* or *no*.

1. Is Han Na going to open an account?

   yes   no

2. Is Han Na going to go shopping?

   yes   no

3. Is Han Na going to pay her bills?

   yes   no

Chapter 2

I Open My Accounts

"So, Ms. Park," Mr. Lombardi says, "you want to open two accounts. First, I need your ID."

Mr. Lombardi gives me papers to sign. I have to sign my name many times! Then he types my name and address into his computer.

"Where do you work, Ms. Park?" he asks.

"I'm the cook at the Korean restaurant on the corner," I say.

"I know that restaurant!" he says. "I often eat lunch there."

Mr. Lombardi shows me different styles of checks. I choose green. The bank is going to print my name, address, and account number on my checks.

"Can I get my checks today?" I ask.

"No," he says. "You're going to get them in the mail. Your bank statements also come in the mail every month. They tell you your balances."

"A balance is how much money is in my account, right?" I ask.

"Right," says Mr. Lombardi.

"Can I deposit my check now?" I ask.

"Sure," says Mr. Lombardi.

I give my check to Mr. Lombardi.

"Excuse me," he says. He leaves his desk for a few minutes. Then he comes back and gives me a piece of paper.

"This is your receipt," he says. "It shows the amount of your deposit and your balance."

Then I ask, "Can my employer deposit my paychecks electronically?"

"Oh, that's easy," says Mr. Lombardi. "Write VOID on one of your checks and give it to him."

"OK," I say.

Mr. Lombardi shows me how I can bank online. I move some money into my savings account. I can also pay my bills.

Then I remember. I need some cash.

"Can I withdraw some cash now?" I ask.

"Yes," says Mr. Lombardi. "You can withdraw cash from the ATM."

"Oh!" I say. "How do I use the ATM?"

A. These sentences are false. Make them true.

1. Mr. Lombardi often eats breakfast at the Korean restaurant.

   <u>Mr. Lombardi often eats lunch at the Korean restaurant.</u>

2. Han Na is going to get her checks today.

3. Han Na cashes her check.

4. Han Na knows how to use the ATM.

B. Complete the sentences. Use the words in the box.

ATM	~~balance~~	bank online
bank statement	receipt	

1. Your _____<u>balance</u>_____ is how much money you have in your account.

2. You need a computer to _____ .

3. You can use the _____ to withdraw money from your account.

4. I deposit $100 into my account. The teller hands me a _____ .

5. Your _____ comes in the mail every month.

C. Organize information. What does Han Na do at the bank? Write 3 or 4 sentences. Make sure they are in the correct order.

<u>Han Na meets a teller named Felicia.</u>

**What's going to happen next? What do you think?
Read the question. Then circle your guess, *yes* or *no*.**

1. Is Han Na going to deposit
   another check into her
   account?
   yes   no

3. Is Han Na going to work at
   the bank?
   yes   no

2. Is Han Na going to get an
   ATM card?
   yes   no

4. Is Felicia going to eat lunch at
   the restaurant?
   yes   no

Chapter 3

I Get an ATM Card

"You need an ATM card," says Mr. Lombardi. He gives me a plastic card. I sign the back. He tells me I'm going to get a new card with my name on it.

Mr. Lombardi tells me I also need a PIN. He asks me to choose a number I can remember.

"Should I write it down?" I ask.

"No," he says. "And never tell anyone your PIN."

I hope I don't forget my PIN!

NEW BANK

This ATM charges a fee of $1.50.
Do you want to continue?

YES   **NO**

"Can I use any ATM?" I ask.

"You can, Ms. Park," he says. "There are many ATMs in town. But at other banks you have to pay a fee for the ATM. Only the Town Bank ATMs are free. That's because you have an account here."

"There's an ATM at my restaurant," I say. "Do I have to pay a fee at that one?"

"Yes," he says. "You have to pay a fee at that ATM."

"Can I deposit money at the ATM?" I ask.

"Yes, you can, Ms. Park," says Mr. Lombardi. "You enter your PIN. Then you put the money or the check into an envelope. You put the envelope into the ATM. The ATM gives you a receipt with your balance."

"That sounds easy," I say. "And how do I withdraw cash?"

"You enter your PIN. Then you choose *withdraw*, the account, and the amount."

"I can show you how to use the ATM now," says Mr. Lombardi. "Is there anything else I can help you with today?"

"No," I say. "I have a checking account. I have a savings account. I know how to bank online. I have an ATM card. And my checks are going to come in the mail. I think that's everything."

"Good," says Mr. Lombardi.

I smile. "I'm ready to try the ATM!" I say.

New
Accounts

A. Choose the correct answer.

1. Han Na signs the back of her ____ .

    a. ATM card
    b. check
    c. bank statement

2. Han Na needs a PIN to ____ .

    a. open an account
    b. get her checks in the mail
    c. use the ATM

3. Han Na can use an envelope to ____ .

    a. mail her check
    b. deposit a check in the ATM
    c. withdraw cash

B. Circle the correct word.

1. I don't know how to (bank / sign) online.

2. He's going to (pay / deposit) his bills online.

3. (Choose / Sign) your credit card right away.

4. At the ATM, you (enter / choose) your PIN.

5. This isn't my bank. I need to (enter / pay) a fee at the ATM.

6. He needs money today. He's going to (deposit / withdraw) $100 in cash.

C. Organize information. How can Han Na deposit a check at the ATM? Write 3 or 4 sentences. Make sure they are in the correct order.

What's going to happen next? What do you think? Read the question. Then circle your guess, *yes* or *no*.

1. Is Han Na going to deposit money in her savings account?
   yes   no

3. Is Han Na going to withdraw cash from the ATM?
   yes   no

2. Is Han Na going to take a trip to Korea?
   yes   no

4. Are Han Na and Mr. Lombardi going to go to the restaurant?
   yes   no

21

Chapter 4

I Use the ATM

"OK, Ms. Park," says Mr. Lombardi. "Let's go to the ATM."

We walk to the ATM. We wait for a minute because there's another customer using it.

"Do you remember your PIN?" Mr. Lombardi asks.

I do, but I'm nervous. "What happens if I push the wrong button?" I ask.

"Don't worry," says Mr. Lombardi. "You can fix it!"

I laugh. I don't feel nervous now.

1.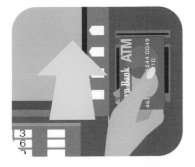

3.

2.

4.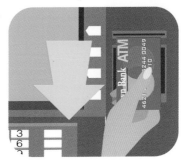

The other customer leaves.

"Let's begin," says Mr. Lombardi.

I read the words on the screen. Mr. Lombardi tells me what some of the words mean.

I insert my ATM card and enter my PIN. I choose how much cash I want. I take the cash and remove my card.

Then the ATM gives me a receipt. I put the money, the receipt, and my ATM card in my wallet.

That was easy!

"Do the same thing when you deposit money," says Mr. Lombardi. "Read the words on the screen. Choose *deposit*. Then choose one of your accounts, savings or checking."

He points to the envelopes. "Here are the envelopes. Put your check or cash inside."

"That's easy!" I say. "I feel better now."

"Thank you for helping me, Mr. Lombardi," I say.

"You're welcome, Ms. Park," he says.

"I have to go now," I say. "Tomorrow the lunch special is tofu soup. I have to buy more tofu."

"Good!" says Mr. Lombardi. "I love the tofu soup. It's my favorite lunch. I think I want tofu soup for lunch tomorrow."

"See you soon, then!" I say.

What a busy morning!

A. Mark the sentences true (T) or false (F). Change the false sentences. Make them true.

_F_ **1.** Han Na uses the ATM at her restaurant.

   Han Na uses the ATM at the bank,

____ **2.** Han Na gets a receipt from Mr. Lombardi.

____ **3.** Han Na puts her ATM card in her wallet.

____ **4.** Han Na gives her money to Mr. Lombardi.

____ **5.** Mr. Lombardi shows Han Na where the envelopes are.

B. Label the pictures. Use the words in the box.

choose the account	insert my ATM card
remove my card	take the cash

1.

_____

3.

_____

2.

_____

4.

_____

C. Organize information. Look at the poster. Check (✓) the correct sentences.

At Town Bank, you can

_____ 1. learn how to bank online.

_____ 2. buy postage stamps.

_____ 3. use an ATM.

_____ 4. send email.

_____ 5. learn how to save money.

_____ 6. open a checking account.

What's Next?

Think about what Han Na is going to do now. Write 2 or 3 sentences.

After Reading Activity

A. Use the Internet.

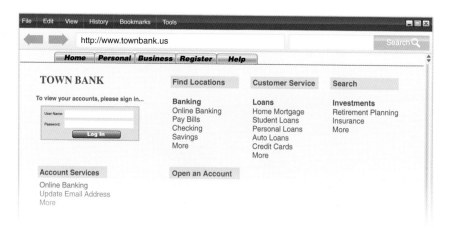

- Look at the website for Town Bank.
- What services does Town Bank offer?

B. Work with a partner. Find information about a bank.

- Look up *banks* on the Internet.
- Find a bank near your home.
- Make a list of the services the bank offers.
- Share your list with your class.
- Make a class list of banks. Put them in alphabetical order by name.
- Put a star next to the banks in your neighborhood.

Useful Expressions

apply for a credit card	open an account
apply for a loan	view your accounts
online banking	

Shared vocabulary from the *OPD*
and *A Busy Morning at the Bank*

account manager
[ə kownt/ măn/ə jər]

ATM
[ā/tē/ĕm/]

ATM card
[ā/tē/ĕm/ kärd/]

balance
[băl/əns]

bank online
[băngk/ än līn/]

bank statement
[băngk/ stāt/mənt]

check
[chĕk]

checking account
[chĕk/ĭng ə kownt/]

cook
[kook]

customer
[kŭs/tə mər]

deposit
[dĭ päz/ət]

enter your PIN
[ĕn/tər yər pĭn/]

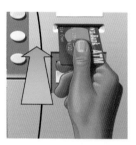

insert your ATM card
[ĭn sürt/ yər ā/tē/ĕm/ kärd/]

remove your card
[rĭ mōōv/ yər kärd/]

restaurant
[rĕs/tə rənt]

savings account
[sā/vĭngz ə kownt/]

teller
[tĕl/ər]

withdraw
[wĭdh drö/]